# Cybronics

# Cybronics

## Our Online Language

*Jordan Plieskatt*

Writers Club Press
San Jose  New York  Lincoln  Shanghai

**Cybronics**
**Our Online Language**

Writers Club Press
an imprint of iUniverse.com, Inc.


For information address:
iUniverse.com, Inc.
5220 S 16th, Ste. 200
Lincoln, NE 68512
www.iuniverse.com


ISBN: 0-595-17877-4

Printed in the United States of America

# CONTENTS

v

## TIPS

# PREFACE

Cybronics, the online language, was developed through years of trial and error by many internet users. In the past, there has never been a standardized set of terms for users online. Cybronics is far from a set vocabulary or language. It is rather a method. Some useful examples are presented to the user in this text. The purpose of such a language arose out of many years of complications with the use standard or textbook English online. Perhaps the most valuable aspect of Cybronics is its ease of use for the online world. Cybronics is simply our common English brought into a new reality, cyberspace. It is an adaptation of the English language through manipulations of spelling for use online.

When users first encounter the online world they tend to use proper English. After time, it tends to become awkward and a hassle. An online world has many demands. One of which is the ability to respond quickly and to carry on a conversation rapidly. The problem most users encounter is time. Since a typed message is seldom in real-time, there is a need to have quick responses to questions posted online. Proper English has many boundaries that cause users to ramble on aimlessly and wastefully. When online, one has to get to the point quickly, and do so by the quickest route. Eventually, due to typos by the user, abbreviations or misspellings become the norm. Typos are ignored and soon they make sense to the recipient of the message. If it comes close to what it is suppose to say, there is no need for correction. This eventually evolves from typos into purposely made grammar mistakes in order to type faster. Soon dropping the last few letters of a word makes sense and changing vowels are okay.

All languages experience evolution. They evolve to become more efficient and to adapt to the new age of man itself. The online world is always evolving too. The goal is to make this online world unique and efficient. The online world is an ever-changing world. With change, comes new ideas to suite this developing world. Cybronics suits the online world and its users perfectly.

People have even come up with the idea and methods of expressing feelings and actions through characters. These are not words of description, but rather keyboard characters and words manipulated into a symbol for an action. This allows the users a humorous approach to their emotions online. Due to the wide connectivity of the Internet, this new "language" is frequently shared among users. To <<net gods>>, longtime, revered Internet users, this becomes a common and apt language. To people outside cyberspace, the Cybronics language might seem to be nonsense. Yet, the objective of Cybronics is to make sense. This language was developed from real users. Cybronics is not a "test tube language," nor a language that was researched and developed; it is developed by common usage. Real online users created this, and the rest of the users might like to be made aware of such a language. This book was written by watching users chat and it is how the authors talk online. Most importantly, this book shows to the <<newbies>>, unfamiliar or new Internet users, how to adopt this language into common use. Countries have their own unique languages. The online country now has its own distinctive language - Cybronics.

Cybronics is not to be abused. There is a specific time and place (The online world) in which it should be used. The important rule is to use discretion. There are things that work fine with the English language. Newspapers and T.V. use English on an everyday basis, and it works. Even so, there has been an extent of abuse to the English language. " Slang" is a corruption of the English language. Granted, corruption is far from avoidable, but it can be delayed and controlled. There is no need to change a good thing. The rules are simple: If it looks right and seems right, it is right. Have fun with Cybronics. It is a fun and distinct language. There are no textbooks to study or quizzes to pass. Here a few methods to get one on the path to understanding the language of the online world.

The Warning: This does not mean to give up studying English and to use this language in writing school papers. Do not abuse this short-cut. This gift is given to online users to allow their transmission of ideas to become prompt. English is the language we use in the public, a language society has created and manipulated to be proper. The online world is not suitable for such a language. There is call for a unique language to the Internet. And Cybronics is the answer. The message is to not abuse this. Put your school-educated language to use in reality. And leave virtual reality and Cybronics for those on the information frontier. It is a shame there has already been corruption and abuse to the online world. Cybronics is not a corruption, but rather a distinction. It is the distinct language of the online world. Real users in real time, online, use it. In today's age, old is out and new is in. Cybronics is the new. It meets the demand of cyberspace.

# CUTTIN THE WERDZ SHORT

## DROPPIN THE G

The English language is full of rules and restrictions. This presents us with many complications. There are rules for distinction of the tense of a verb. These rules tell how to conjugate a verb into the proper tense. One tense is the present participle. When forming the present participle, an "ing" is added. "Sailing" is an example of this tense. When "ing" is used as a suffix, it creates an action or process. The present participle is an example of the proper English language.

Cybronics eliminates a few letters. The ending letter "g" is dropped from the suffix. This is done for many reasons. First, it shortens the word. One less letter can make it a lot easier and faster to type over a period of time. When a user combines this change with others, one can shorten words even more and cause greater ease of use.

*Example*
"Sailing" now becomes " sailin."

The second justification for dropping the "g" is that the ending "g" is never pronounced nor heard. English spelling can be confusing. Words are often ended or begun with a letter that has no relevancy to its pronunciation.

For what ever reason, dropping the "g" makes the online chat a little more user friendly. It is possibly the easiest concept to learn. Soon droppin the "g" becomes natural and convenient. A few examples of the use of this concept are listed here. Again, this is an online concept and is not meant to replace proper English grammar anywhere else but online.

*Examples of Droppin the G:*

| | | |
|---|---|---|
| Doing | becomes | Doin |
| Working | becomes | Workin |
| Showing | becomes | Showin |
| Rowing | becomes | rowin |

*Conversation examples:*
**User1:** whatcha *doin?*
**User2:** *nuttin* much…just *talkin* to ya.
**User3:** T's kewl…I'm just *workin* on some graphix.

# CUTTIN THE WERDZ SHORT CONT'D

## DROPPIN THE BEGINNING

There are many objectives in having Cybronics. Cybronics is not only a useful language, but also a unique one. With such a language, a user can have as much fun with it as the user wants. Dropping the beginning of a word is just an unusual twist to Cybronics. This is not done on a regular basis, due to the chance of confusion. In a few instances, though, it adds an oddity to the language.

*Examples*

- In an online conversation one can use "round" as one would use "around."

**User1**: I'm leavin *round* 3.

This is justifiable because the person is not going to confuse the connotation. The person understands in this instance that "round" means "around."

- Another example is using "cause" in place of "because".

**User2**: I left *cause* I was bored.

Again, the recipient of the message understands that "cause" is supposed to mean "because". In this instance it has saved typing two letters. Over time, two less letters can put one further ahead and save time

• A third example of dropping the beginning is " bout."

**User1:** I was there *bout* 4pm.

Here, "bout" obviously means "about". This not only is one less letter but an interesting attribute to a conversation.

• Other examples include using "least" in place of "at least."

Again, don't go overboard. There is no need to constantly drop prefixes or the beginning letters of words. Users should use discretion. Dropping the beginning not only allows one to type faster, but also a rare twist to a conversation and Cybronics.

# THE LETTERS X & Z

## *MAKE' EM LOOK LIKE THEY SOUND*

Sometimes Cybronics may not look anything close to English. A user knows he is really using Cybronics when he starts adding letters to make it look interesting. What is even more interesting is that making them look neat also makes them look how they sound. When one thinks of the consonant and its sound, it may not always make sense in English. A good example is the word "phone." Realistically one should spell "phone" "fone." Our English language, however, replaces the "f" sound with a "ph." In Cybronics, the spelling of "phone" would simply be "fone." Another example is "was." In the online language a user would spell "was," by changing the "s" to a "z." "Was" now becomes "waz." Cybronics makes them look like they sound. A few examples have been listed below:

*Examples*

Let's take " thanks" for example. In Cybronics "thanks" is simply spelled "thanx." Both are pronounced the same way. Both still contain the same meaning. One is just revised. This revision adds uniqueness to it, and it replaces the sound of two letters with one letter.

A second example is replacing an "s" with a "z." A user should not replace every "s" with a "z," just replace the ending consonant. Most often this is used in the plural form. Cybronics, instead of using an "s" uses a "z" in the plural form. This concept is mot often used in bringing attention to one's words. It presents the message, "Hey, this is plural!" Below, are a few examples and their correct spellings:

*More Examples*

| Words | becomes | Wordz |
| Days | becomes | Dayz |
| Socks | becomes | Sox |

Use this method sparingly. This method can get a little confusing at times. A user should just use this periodically to add emphasis or to add an uncommon twist to the conversation.

# MAKING THE WERDZ LOOK EVEN BETTER

## PLAYING AROUND WITH VOWELS

The Internet is a beloved second home to many users. One should think of the Internet as a bare room. Cybronics simply starts to decorate that room. Each method creates a new picture for a blank wall. A concept adds some furniture to that home and makes it seem a little more comfortable to the user. Cybronics decorates this world in its own unusual way. The user chooses how much decoration he wants by controlling how much he applies the online language.

When a user presents himself to the point where he changes vowels of words, he can be sure he has added a lot of decoration to that room. The changing of vowels is just simply "playin around." There is no method to it. A user is just having fun with this concept. He is supposed to make the words look as abstract as he wants. Included are some examples of how some users change vowels. One is just to try to pick a new vowel with a sound similar to the original. An added bonus is that sometimes a user replaces two vowels with one. This brings us back to the concept of short and concise. The shorter the word, the better it is.

### Examples

| Word | becomes | Werd |
|------|---------|------|
| Your | becomes | Yer |

| Cool | becomes | Kewl |
|------|---------|------|
| Love | becomes | Luv |
| For | becomes | Fer |
| Yourself | becomes | Yerself |
| Are | becomes | R |
| Enough | becomes | Enuf (an example of vowel and conso- nant change) |

Most often "ou" or "i" sounds are replaced with an "e." The idea, here, is to add a twist and originality to your "werdz." A thought to remember though: The idea is not to put too much furniture into this room. A user should not crowd the room with furniture, so that he cannot move about freely. One should add "enuf" furniture, though, so that he may sit down and be comfortable.

# ::ACTIONS::

## *GETTIN YER POINT ACROSS ONLINE*

When a user is online he is transmitting through text. The transmission of text, rather than video presents a problem. It leaves it hard to "see" a users actions, expression, or personality. In Cybronics, a user relies on words to express his or her actions and feelings through several methods. The online language replaces a group of words with symbols or characters. Four full colons placed on either side of the verb replaces the phrase "I am,".

A user may now use ::*term*:: in place of an expression. "I am distracted" now becomes "::Distracted::." This often comes in handy. In Cybronics, grouping is far shorter than typing out a full sentence. A very popular Cybronics grouping is "::Sigh::." The people who are annoyed and agitated at another user tend to do this when they get disgusted in a chat session. ::Sigh:: is truly a particular twist to the Cybronics vocabulary.

### *Examples*

| | | |
|---|---|---|
| I am smiling | becomes | ::Smiling:: |
| I am looking at you suspiciously | becomes | ::Looks at u suspiciously:: |
| I am grinning | becomes | ::Grins:: |

Any action can now be placed in full colons to take the place of a full sentence. The more aggressive users tend to use this method. The idea is to offer a concise option to expressing ones actions.

For someone who is being ignored in a chat room:
::Sits down in comfy chair and waits::
The idea here is one can personalize it and use this trait freely and as frequently as one likes.

The full colon method does not only have to be applied to actions and expressions. In Cybronics, a user may use the full colons to represent an adjective. This adjective normally describes the user talking. Again, rather than saying, "I am smart." A user may now just type " ::smart::." This is a fun method because it allows a user to compliment himself in a unrivaled way.

There are other methods of expressing adjectives as well. A user might also type an arrow pointing at their name and the adjective following to describe him. The examples below show two methods. It is a rather simple process once one gets the hang of it.

T
### Additional Examples

*The original and full colon method:*
**User1:** I am smart
This can then be replaced with
**User1:** ::Smart::

*The original and arrow method:*
**User2:** I am smart
This is then replaced with

**User2:** <- - Smart

A third application of this technique is used when exiting a conversation. A user can add his own specific trademark to his exit. The examples below present some exit methods.

*The old traditional English way:*
**User1:** I am leaving

*The semi-advanced Cybronics way:*
**User1:** ::Exits::
    or
**User2:** ::Leaves::
*The way the masters do it:*
**User:** ::Evaporates::
This is just a fancy and classy exit routine.

When using full colons have fun with it. Some users tend to use six full colons rather than the four mentioned here. Either way is acceptable. This is a technique that can never be overdone. The more you use it, the better. A user will find out that it makes conversations go much faster. First, it cuts down on the number of words to type when using this method. It also presents the message: "Hey! I know Cybronics!"

# Expressin Yer Thoughts

## *Make' em See What Ya Feel*

Users not only want to express actions online, but convey feelings as well. A lot of times, a user will find himself feeling something that has no English spelling. In this chapter you will find some of the most commonly used online terms. Whatever one is feeling, there is a Cybronics word for it. One may use these terms as often as he likes. What a user feels, he should say. The terms below are simply just what say.

First, a user should know what to say when he does not have any words to contribute to the conversation. The first example is the Cybronics term "la." When one is awaiting a response, probably impatiently, one can sing. A user just simply states "la" as many times as needed until attention is brought to himself. To the other user the repetition of "la" on his screen gets pretty annoying. Conversation is sure to continue after this.

Once a user is bored with just using "la," he may combine it with other terms. The expression " la de dum," is a perfect time filler. A user can just say it out of the blue, or if he if is waiting for the conversation to continue. These are just a few terms. A user should just use them whenever he feels compelled to.

Finally, the last boring term is "hmmmm." This term is used when one feels they need to break the ice. "hmmmm?", signifies a question. This is a great conversation starter. A user should feel free to add as many "m's" to "hmmmm" as he wishes. The more the merrier.

Now that a user knows how to fill time he needs to know some more things about how to convey his feelings. Cybronics has many terms for those that are agitated. Below is a list of terms and instructions for the agitated user:

### *Examples*

*Grrrrrrrrr*

A user is to use this term like a dog. If a user wants to growl at another user, "grrrr" is his answer. This term is another popular term with the users. It always seems to add a sense of humor to a conversation. Normally, though, you do not want to imitate an animal. Remember, even online, we are humans.

*Arg*

This term also originated with those imitating an animal. "Arg," has many connotations. One connotation is a question. When someone responds with "arg," he is normally questioning something. In this case, "arg," has the same connotation as "::looking at someone questioningly::." Other connotations include that of agitation. "Arg" may bring across the feeling that one is not pleased. Again, feel free to use this term to its full extent. Dictionary definitions are not needed to convey the meaning.

*Ewwwwwww*

This, obviously, has to do with one being disgusted. Just like a little child might say "ewwwww" to his vegetables. An online user expresses his unhappiness much the same way. (This term is normally still used on the topic of food online.)

*Ack*

This is possibly one of the most original terms online. A user presents the word "ack," when he is surprised. Normally, the surprise is not appreciated nor expected.

**User1:** I just lost $500

**User2:** *Ack*! That's a lot of money

*Uh huh*

This term is a jewel. Those users expressing disbelief use it most regularly. This term also connotes the idea of suspicion towards the other user.

**User1:** I just won a million dollars

**User2:** *uh huh*…sure ya did User1

Now that the abstract terms are covered, let us move onto laughing. There are many ways of expressing humorous actions online. In the next chapter, "Abbreviations," one will find a few laughs. Those that actually want to imitate their real life laugh online should read on.

*Examples*

"Heh" is a simple basic laugh online. If something is said that is moderately funny one may respond with "heh."

"Hehe" is an imitation of a high-pitched annoying laugh. A user that acts obnoxiously online loves this one. After a sarcastic remark, "hehe," often finds its place.

"Hehehehehehehehehehe" is an ongoing laugh. This phrase is left for the highly humorous incidents online.

"Muahaha" is for the evil people out there. It imitates the evil, devilish cackle of some people.

Whatever one wants to express, Cybronics has a way to express it. The few terms mentioned are just the beginning. Again, there is no set vocabulary to the online world. Cybronics challenges those to go out and create anew. A user is not to go overboard and appear abstract to others. Users want to be original, not inane and confusing to others.

# ABBREVIATIONS

## *THE SHORTER THE BETTER*

This chapter is dedicated to all the confused <<newbies>> of
the online world.

In an online chat a user might hear the ever popular, "What does LoL
mean?" This phrase or question is normally presented by a confused
newbie. (A newbie is a person new to the online environment). This
little newbie might have found himself right in the midst of a
Cybronics discussion. Most newbies find out the Cybronics abbreviations through such embarrassing questions. Well, to give the newbie
a head start, a list has been compiled. Hopefully such foresight will
save the newbie any further embarrassment.

On the contrary, abbreviations are not created to confuse the dis-
traught newbie. (Although, it is an added bonus to those familiar with
the online world.) Abbreviations are created for greater ease of use
online. They take the place of a word or phrase that would normally
occupy a lot of space. Abbreviations are just a further example of the
versatility of Cybronics. They are to be used whenever possible and
applicable. One, however, should not create abstract abbreviations. The
idea here is to have abbreviations that are easily definable and recogniz-
able to the other user. It is simply just a shortcut for the Cybronics user.

The abbreviations listed in this chapter were created because of the practicality of them and should be used as often as the user wants to. Each abbreviation is followed by a brief explanation.

## *Examples*

*Sup*  This word takes the place of the question, "What is up?" This word is frequently used among users in chat. This term enables familiar users to simply ask what the other is doing or feeling.

*F & M*  These letters simply replaces one sex. In chat one might ask "age/sex?" The other user would respond with simply his age and "m" for male or "f" for female. Four or six letters are now replaced with one.
**User1:** 19/m

*J/k*  This is a frequently used abbreviation addressing the topic of humor. One would say "j/k" in place of "joking." This abbreviation comes in handy for replacing an entire word relating to humor.

*NE*  These two letters can mean a lot. The sounds of both letters combine to sound a bit like "any." This is the character's meaning. "NE" can be followed by other abbreviations to mean other words. This is a very useful abbreviation with many applications.

| Anytime | becomes | NEtime |
| Anything | becomes | NEthing |
| Anywhere | becomes | NEwhere |

*1* "1" simply replaces the word "one" or "won." Here, a numeric character replaces a word.

One may now combine the two terms above to form other abbreviations and meanings:

Anyone    becomes    NE1


*2* "2" replaces either of three words: "to," "too," "two." Of course, any numeric number may replace its title word. This is just one example, however, with other meanings:

go to go    becomes    g2g

User2:I am goin 2 the mall

User1:Well, I g2g


*U*        The one character "u" can be used to replace the entire word "you."


*R*        The letter "r" replaces the word "are."

        Combining the above terms can be very efficient.

User1: R U There?


*Pic*        The Cybronics word "Pic," replaces the word "picture." This is frequently used in chat. It is most often used to ask for ones picture. The plural of "pic" is "pix."

User2: Do you have a pic?

*Additional Examples*

AkA        Also known as

AFK        Away from keyboard

BRB        Be right back

BTW        By the way

G2g        Got to go

| | |
|---|---|
| GMTA | Great minds think alike (Great for complimenting oneself) |
| K | Means "ok," or "yes." |
| KW | Means keyword (used on AOL) |
| LoL | Laugh out loud (another abbreviation to replace laughter) |
| ROFL | Rolling on floor laughing (Not for the mildly humorous chats) |
| SN | means the screen name of a person |
| SR | System Responds |
| WB | Welcome back |

As long as the abbreviation makes sense and is easily decipherable, use it, or create it.

# ANSWERS

## HOW TO ANSWER IN CYBRONICS

This chapter is for anyone who is tired of hearing
"yeah" in public.

Cybronics offers a number of solutions to the English slang
dilemma. Basically, in English slang there are two improper answers:
"yeah" and "neah ." Cybronics gives users several alternatives.

Any users disgusted with "yeah," now have seven positive alternatives. All in all, the most proper response is "yes." But, there are
those users that challenge the norm. The first alternative is "yup."
"Yup" is your basic "yes" online. From "yup," one can then change it
to "yupper," and so on. Below are some basic positive responses.

*Examples*

*Positive responses:*
Ah
K
Ya
Yah
Yeah
Yessum
Yup

Yupper
(The ever unpopular) Yes


Now that a user knows how to respond positively, he also needs to know how to respond negatively. The basic negative response is simply "no." The English slang response is "neah." The list below has some more Cybronics answers.

*Examples*

*Negative responses:*
Nah
Neah
No (Very unpopular)
Nope
Noper
Nuttin


Cybronics aims for originality. These methods of response are just some more ways to create a more interesting online experience.

# CAPS

## GETTIN YER POINT ACROSS WITH BIG LETTERS (YELLING)

Now that a user knows most of the basics, he needs to know how to convey some of his strong feelings. Basically this is called yelling. This chapter will deal with how one would yell at someone online. Since it is rather hard to convey a louder tone through text, some text attributes have to apply for this purpose. There are two ways of conveying yelling, both of which will be described below.

The first, and most common technique of yelling is using the caps lock key. The capital letter signifies a louder tone to the user online. It provides emphasis. Examples are below.

**User1:** HOW COULD U

**User2:** DON'T YELL AT ME

Of course, there is the time when someone hits the caps lock key by accident. This is sometimes confusing to the other user and normally requires an apology.

**User1:** I LEAVIN AT 6

**User2:** Why so angry?

**User1:** Ack…caps…sorry

The caps key does not always signify anger. Capital letters are also used to draw attention to the user's words. Just make sure the correct connotation is inferred.

The second method of yelling online requires larger letters. One can simply increase the font size to simulate a louder tone of voice.

**User1:** WB

**User2:** Thanx

Whichever method one chooses, he should make sure to use it properly. A user can really anger another fairly easily by miscommunication. A user should use other Cybronics words to make sure he conveys his message clearly to others.

# GETTING THE LINGO DOWN

## ADDING SOME LETTERZ

Once a user has the basic steps done he can really start to have fun. The methods mentioned before are the basics. From the basics, one can start to create his own techniques. The idea is not to be abstract. A user can take some chances, but be reserved too. A few personal methods are mentioned below.

"T" is a great letter to add. It adds an interesting pronunciation and touch to your Cybronics. The majority of the time "t" precedes the English word.

**User1:** T'was interesting

**User2:** correct

With Cybronics, it is an open language. A user should be able to make it personal. The language is totally open to changes and adaptations.

Cybronics: *Use it, Create it*

# GETTING THE LINGO DOWN

## TYPO BATS

Typos are a peculiar twist to the online world. They are an uncommon twist to Cybronics. As mentioned before, much of Cybronics was created from typos made by users in the past. A user should not fret over whether he typed something correctly. A user should be more concerned with what he typed and how he presented it. If typos are made, as they will be, forget about them. About 99% of typos are decipherable. The other 1% may deserve some explanation. No user is error free. A user should laugh about the typos. Most of the time they are funny looking. Cybronics is having fun with the online world and language. Don't let typos ruin your day or Cybronics experience!

# Getting the Lingo Down
## *Type it, but Don't Overdue It!*

As mentioned many times before: *BE CONSERVATIVE*

The methods, here, are presented to the user with their appropriate applications and restrictions. Follow the restrictions on each technique carefully. The idea is to be unique. If you think an idea is too abstract, don't use it! The thing is not to overuse any of the methods. It is always better to be conservative.

The other warning:
(Also seen in the preface)

Cybronics is adapted for the online world. This does not mean it is applicable in reality. It is far from applicable in schooling and proper English. Save the Cybronics for the Internet. The world in which we live is centered on our English. This world is far from being suited for a dramatic change. The change is needed online. Use Cybronics online. A user should have fun with Cybronics, online that is.

# TIPS

## *Now Ya Know*

(Mostly AOL):

- Don't give your password to anyone, including AOL.

- The only places you should ever type your password are the setup and sign-on box, and KW password (when you want to change it.)

- Go to KW TOS to learn the terms of service. The terms of service are what you agreed to follow when you signed onto AOL. If you don't follow them your account can be terminated.

- The scrolling limit in chat is set around five lines, if you go over this AOL (bot) will throw you offline.

- If you want to go somewhere, but you don't know how, go to Keyword *Keywords*. Or go to KW "aol://4344:204.keywords.83834.494049278"

- "$IM_off," when typed in your IM "to:" box, turns your IMs off. "$IM_on" turns them on.

- You can have up to four additional screen names on your account. Go to KW *screen name* to activate them.

- It's against TOS(Terms of Service; see KW: TOS) to use vulgarities in chat.

- To find out if someone has read the mail you sent to them, open the "sent mail" window and click on "status" with the desired mail highlighted.

- To ignore someone in chat, click on their name, and click the ignore button in the information box.

- To make a hypertext link in your mail, click the "format" button. On the bar that appears, click the "insert" button, and insert your link.

- Call America Online at 1-800-827-6364.

- To blind copy your mail, when mailing to more than one person, click the arrow next to the "to" icon (in the "address to" box,) and select "BCC." This way, the recipient of the mail cannot see who was on the list other than him/herself.

- To report TOS violations go to KW "TOS." You can also Email TOS violations or concerns to the following:
TOSGeneral
TOSEmail1
TOSIM1
TOS Files

- To roll dice in a chatroom: type "//roll." This feature is used in chat, usually in a game amongst other users to see who can get a higher total.

- Online host is not a person, it's a bot triggered by the "//" command and the "=q" command.

- No stalking, death threats, etc. TOS doesn't like it when you threaten people. However, some people can get away with a lot.

- Guides and hosts are people you can talk to them and you can make them angry, if there are no real "set in stone" rules with them.

- You can respond to any warning AOL gives you. AKA (also known as) if you have broken TOS accidentally and they catch you on it you can explain what happened to them.

- People on AOL do mail bomb, try to steal your account, etc. Be careful and respectful of those that have more online knowledge.

- AOL records credit card numbers's and SN's . . .you can't use them twice. You can now reactivate old screen names.

- TOS is also against masked vulgarity (such as a$$ or F&*^%) They also don't like slang vulgarity (such as askhole, fukk.)

- You have only violated TOS when you get a "you have violated" email.

- AOL records violations.

- Click on the little heart in the corner of your windows to have that window recorded as a "favorite place."

- To create your own member room (without having to go through KW "chat") you can enter KW "aol://2719:62-2-" followed by the name of the room.

- If you want privacy, you can create a private room using KW "aol://2719:2-2-" followed by the room name. There you are placed in an environment that will be non-offensive to other users.

- Get virus protection software at KW "virus."

- Get other software for your computer at KW "Files"

- If you are dialing up AOL, you may receive a busy signal during "peak hours." It normally gets better around 2 or 3 AM.

- AOL signs you off after 10 minutes of inactivity.

- By writing mail offline you save valuable phone time and possibly money. All you have to do is choose "compose mail" while offline.

# FACES

## *PLASTIC SURGERY FOR THE ONLINE WORLD*

The online world, as mentioned before, presents many technicalities that are hard to get around. One of those technicalities is using text rather than video. Cybronics now offers solution for this with some visual aid, specifically faces and pictures.

A user's basic face is a pair of eyes and a mouth. A user normally coordinates his faces with the moods or feelings he is having at the time. Included are the basic faces and their meaning. (It helps to tilt ones head to the left)

*Examples*

| | |
|---|---|
| =) | The basic smiley face |
| =( | The basic frown face |
| =[ | A version of a frown |
| =] | A kind of dumb smirk looking face |
| ={ | A grumbled frowny face |
| =} | Just an odd looking smile |
| =\ | The hurt feeling look |
| =/ | The unhappy look |
| =\| | The not-amused look |
| =0 | Just a big open mouth |

| | |
|---|---|
| =o | A surprised face |
| =O | This is either a yell or a yawn |
| =P | A face sticking tongue out |
| =b | Another tongue sticker |
| => | The weird smile |
| =< | The unhappy guy |
| =? | The questioning look |
| =B | A buck tooth |
| =I | Either a sour looking face or a not amused look |
| =D | The big happy grin |
| =S | Use your imagination |
| =* | A kiss |
| =X | This means lips-are-sealed |

From the basic faces seen above other traits can be added to the face. The next feature to use would be eyebrows. The eyebrow examples are presented below:

>=)             or              <=)

A user should use whatever eyebrow he feels best suites the situation

A user has other options, of course, for eyes. There are about seven different eyes one can use on the faces.

*Examples*

: + mouth                    These are just smaller eyes.

*Example:*    : )
; + mouth                                     This normally signifies a wink.
*Example:*    ; )
8 + mouth                                     These are big bug-eyes.
*Example:*    8 )
B + mouth                                     This is a face wearing sunglasses.
*Example:*    B )
0 + mouth                                     This is the ever-popular Cyclops.
*Example:*    0 )

The next step to add to the face is a nose. There are three options available for the noses on virtual faces:

=^ )                          This is the ever-popular pointy nose.
=o )                          This is the typical clown nose added to
                              a face.
=- )                          This is the smaller nose.

The final step and addition to the face is hair. For hair there are not many options. The current hair styles are presented below.

§=)                          A face with curly hair
| = )                        A face with flat top hair
{ =)                         A Toupee.
[ =)                         A major-side burns head.

Cybronics users have also created some unique faces and other pictures:

## Examples

| | |
|---|---|
| (ô¿ô) | These combined characters form a complete face |
| x P | The Mr. Yuk face |
| =)-~ | A face smoking a cigarette |
| @@@@:) | The Marge Simpson look |
| (•..•) | Alien #1 |
| (<>..<>) | Alien #2 |
| =: | This is supposed to be an ant |
| o-)-<]: | A skater boarder sideways (sk8ter in Cybronics) |
| =)-/-< | A full representation of a person |
| ————=========(() | This can be deciphered as a marshmallow flying |
| <————<<< | An arrow |
| (:::[ ]:::) | A Band-Aid |
| <>< | A fish (phish) |
| </////////>~ | A joint |
| @)—->———- | A rose |
| ————-{_} | This is a bar mug |
| c[_] | Another mug |

Internet users need to use their imaginations to read the meanings. A lot of creativity by users developed these basic symbols. The majority of the symbols are sideways, and a user has to be able to recognize that. The more faces the merrier. A user can feel free to develop new faces and change old ones. The faces mentioned in this chapter are ones in common usage by the authors.

# WEB PAGES

## *YER OWN LITTLE SPACE ON THE NET*

The Internet has enabled countless opportunities for the general public. Not only does it place various resources at a user's disposal, it allows for users to interact with each other on many levels. One such level is enabling users to create their own web pages.

Web pages can be used for a variety of purposes. If you own your own business, chances are, nowadays you have to be online somehow. Whether it be having a simple page with just contact information or a complete online catalog with ordering features, web pages are essential. Perhaps you are part of an organization and would like to be able to put your information on the Internet to gain support or for resources. The Internet and web pages allow you to do this. On the other hand, many users simply enjoy being able to say they have their own web page. For these purposes, a rather simple page with links, photos, or information is sufficient.

Web pages are usually created using a code. HTML is the most common code used to write web pages. Java scripts and CGI scripts also add some spice to your web page by allowing animations and other special features. The best way to learn HTML is by example. One should surf the Internet and look at web pages. Keep it simple, but keep it interesting. Sometimes too many special features can overwhelm your site visitor. Too little features will make it a boring site, however.

The easiest way to create a web page is to buy a web page composer program. This section, however, will give you the basics and some bits of code to help you to get your website underway.

## The Basics

- index.html—your first page, or home page to the site is the first page websurfers will see. This is usually named "index.html." This page provides basic information and links to other pages of varying topics

- Fonts—The font size, color, and formatting can be changed. Most composers (programs that help you visually create your web page), have simple functions to change your text format

- Images—images can be inserted and used in a variety of fashions. They can simply just be seen on the page, or take on a greater task. A picture can become a link (by clicking on a link, it takes you to a different web page). Images can also be made into image maps, which allow you to link to different pages by clicking on different regions on the same image.

- Indentations and bullets—Your text can be indented or bulleted using dots, graphics, or numbers. This allows an easy method of setting up a list and organizing information.

- Tables—Tables provide an easy method of arranging data on your web page. You do not have to use tables solely for text, but you can also arrange pictures in them. Tables are made up of columns and rows that make a grid on your web page. The width of the lines separating the cells (a specific box in a column and row) can also be changed.

• Justification—Your text can be justified, must like in a word processor. It can be left, center, or right justified.

• Lines—simple lines of varying widths can be used to separate portions of your page. These usually extend the width of the screen.

• Links—text or images can be made into links or hyperlinks. These allow surfers to access other Internet pages from your site by clicking on the text or image. Linked text usually appears underlined.

• Background—The background for your web page can occur in a variety of colors or images can also be used. Changing this option is usually done through "page properties."

## Other Things to Keep in Mind

• Keep things relatively simple in the beginning, use only a few pages with your basics features.

- Keep your web page updated and current. A lot of amateur webmasters tend to setup their page then leave it. Keep adding to it!

- Most websites are made up of multiple pages. To keep confusion to a minimum keep the file names of pages and images short and always use lowercase letters. Using a standard format helps minimize errors.

- Make sure you always have contact information on a website to allow for feedback. This is usually done by listing the webmaster's name and email address at the bottom of the "home" or first page.

- Keep your page well organized with your links. Each page should only address one topic, and then linked to subsequent pages. This allows for easy navigation of the site.

- Check online. You will often find pages that offer free graphics or free bits of code to aid in your website.

Here you will find some sample java scripts. Simply type this code into your <body/> text where you want it to appear to allow for these functions in your web page.

**Java Scripts**
*Clocks, Dates, and Timers*

**Output:** Day, Month date, year (displays current date)

```
<script>

var mydate=new Date()
var year=mydate.getYear()
if (year < 1000)
year+=1900
var day=mydate.getDay()
var month=mydate.getMonth()
var daym=mydate.getDate()
if (daym<10)
daym="0"+daym
var dayarray=new Array("Sunday", "Monday", "Tuesday", "Wednesday", "Thursday",
"Friday", "Saturday")
var montharray=new Array("January", "February", "March", "April", "May", "June",
"July", "August", "September", "October", "November", "December")
document.write("<small><font color='000000' face='Arial'><b>"+dayarray[day]+",
"+montharray[month]+" "+daym+", "+year+"</b></font></small>")

</script>
```

**Output:** date/month/year (displays current date)

```
<script>

var mydate=new Date()
var year=mydate.getYear()
if (year < 1000)
year+=1900
var day=mydate.getDay()
```

```
var month=mydate.getMonth()+1
if (month<10)
month="0"+month
var daym=mydate.getDate()
if (daym<10)
daym="0"+daym
document.write("<small><font color='000000' face='Arial'><b>"+month+"/"+daym+"/
"+year+"</b></font></small>")


</script>
```

## Output: Current time in upper left corner

```
<span id="liveclock" style="position:absolute;left:0;top:0;">
</span>
<script language="JavaScript">
 <!—

function show5(){
if (!document.layers&&!document.all&&!document.getElementById)
return
 var Digital=new Date()
 var hours=Digital.getHours()
 var minutes=Digital.getMinutes()
 var seconds=Digital.getSeconds()
var dn="PM"
if (hours<12)
dn="AM"
if (hours>12)
```

```
hours=hours-12
if (hours==0)
hours=12
 if (minutes<=9)
 minutes="0"+minutes
 if (seconds<=9)
 seconds="0"+seconds
//change font size here to your desire
myclock="<font size='5' face='Arial' ><b><font size='1'>Current Time:</font></br>"
+hours+":"+minutes+":"
 +seconds+" "+dn+"</b></font>"
if (document.layers){
document.layers.liveclock.document.write(myclock)
document.layers.liveclock.document.close()
}
else if (document.all)
liveclock.innerHTML=myclock
else if (document.getElementById)
document.getElementById("liveclock").innerHTML=myclock
setTimeout("show5()",1000)
}
window.onload=show5
//—>
</script>
```

**Output:** displays time in the status bar of the web browser

```
<script language="JavaScript">

        function doClock() {
```

```
window.setTimeout( "doClock()", 1000 );

today = new Date();

self.status = today.toString();
```

```
}
doClock()
</script>
```

## Javascript
### *Fun Scripts*

**Output:** Estimates the number of people on earth at any given moment

```
<script language="JavaScript">


function maind()
{
      startdate = new Date()

now(startdate.getYear(),startdate.getMonth(),startdate.getDate(),startdate.getHours(),startdate.getMinutes(),startdate.getSeconds())
}
```

```
function ChangeValue(number,pv)
{
      numberstring =""
      var j=0
      var i=0
      while (number > 1)
        {

        numberstring = (Math.round(number-0.5) % 10) + numberstring
        number= number / 10
        j++
        if (number > 1 && j==3) {
                        numberstring = "," + numberstring
                        j=0}
        i++
        }

      numberstring=numberstring

if (pv==1) { document.schuld.schuld.value = numberstring }
//if (pv==2) {document.newnow.newnow.value = numberstring}


}




function now(year,month,date,hours,minutes,seconds)
{
      startdatum = new Date(year,month,date,hours,minutes,seconds)
```

```
var now = 5600000000.0
var now2 = 5690000000.0
var groeipercentage = (now2 - now) / now *100
var groeiperseconde = (now * (groeipercentage/100))/365.0/24.0/60.0/60.0
nu = new Date ()
schuldstartdatum = new Date (96,1,1)
secondenoppagina = (nu.getTime() - startdatum.getTime())/1000
totaleschuld= (nu.getTime() - schuldstartdatum.getTime())/1000*groeiperseconde + now
ChangeValue(totaleschuld,1);
//ChangeValue(secondenoppagina*groeiperseconde,2);



    timerID  =  setTimeout("now(startdatum.getYear(),startdatum.getMonth(),startda-
tum.getDate(),startdatum.getHours(),startdatum.getMinutes(),startdatum.getSeconds()
)",200)
    }



window.onload=maind
</script>
```

**The number of people on the planet Earth is now...**

```
<form name="schuld">

<input type="text" name="schuld" size=25 value="">

</FORM>
```

**Output:** Calculates the GPA of a student given certain input

```
<CENTER>
<FORM Name="GPACalcForm">
<TABLE BORDER=5 BGCOLOR=#C0C0C0 CELLPADDING="5"
CELLSPACING="2">
<TH></TH>
<TH>Grade</TH>
<TH>Credits</TH>
<TR>
<TD>Class 1</TD>
<TD><INPUT TYPE=TEXT SIZE=5 NAME="GR1" ALIGN=TOP
MAXLENGTH=5></TD>
<TD><INPUT TYPE=TEXT SIZE=5 NAME="CR1" ALIGN=TOP
MAXLENGTH=5></TD>
</TR>
<TR>
<TD>Class 2</TD>
<TD><INPUT TYPE=TEXT SIZE=5 NAME="GR2" ALIGN=TOP
MAXLENGTH=5></TD>
<TD><INPUT TYPE=TEXT SIZE=5 NAME="CR2" ALIGN=TOP
MAXLENGTH=5></TD>
</TR>
<TR>
<TD>Class 3</TD>
<TD><INPUT TYPE=TEXT SIZE=5 NAME="GR3" ALIGN=TOP
MAXLENGTH=5></TD>
<TD><INPUT TYPE=TEXT SIZE=5 NAME="CR3" ALIGN=TOP
MAXLENGTH=5></TD>
```

```
</TR>
<TR>
<TD>Class 4</TD>
<TD><INPUT TYPE=TEXT SIZE=5 NAME="GR4" ALIGN=TOP
MAXLENGTH=5></TD>
<TD><INPUT TYPE=TEXT SIZE=5 NAME="CR4" ALIGN=TOP
MAXLENGTH=5></TD>
</TR>
<TR>
<TD>Class 5</TD>
<TD><INPUT TYPE=TEXT SIZE=5 NAME="GR5" ALIGN=TOP
MAXLENGTH=5></TD>
<TD><INPUT TYPE=TEXT SIZE=5 NAME="CR5" ALIGN=TOP
MAXLENGTH=5></TD>
</TR>
<TR>
<TD>Class 6</TD>
<TD><INPUT TYPE=TEXT SIZE=5 NAME="GR6" ALIGN=TOP
MAXLENGTH=5></TD>
<TD><INPUT TYPE=TEXT SIZE=5 NAME="CR6" ALIGN=TOP
MAXLENGTH=5></TD>
</TR>
<TR>
<TD>Class 7</TD>
<TD><INPUT TYPE=TEXT SIZE=5 NAME="GR7" ALIGN=TOP
MAXLENGTH=5></TD>
<TD><INPUT TYPE=TEXT SIZE=5 NAME="CR7" ALIGN=TOP
MAXLENGTH=5></TD>
</TR>
<TR>
```

```
<TD>Class 8</TD>
<TD><INPUT TYPE=TEXT SIZE=5 NAME="GR8" ALIGN=TOP
MAXLENGTH=5></TD>
<TD><INPUT TYPE=TEXT SIZE=5 NAME="CR8" ALIGN=TOP
MAXLENGTH=5></TD>
</TR>
<TR ALIGN=CENTER>
<TD COLSPAN=3><INPUT TYPE="BUTTON" VALUE="Calculate"
NAME="CalcButton"
OnClick="gpacalc()"></TD>
</TR>
</TABLE>
</FORM>
<BR>
<P>

<P>
</CENTER>

<BR>


<SCRIPT LANGUAGE="JavaScript">

<!—
function gpacalc()
{
//define valid grades and their values
var gr = new Array(9);
var cr = new Array(9);
```

```
var ingr = new Array(5);
var incr = new Array(5);

// define valid grades and their values
var grcount = 11;
gr[0] = "A+";
cr[0] = 5;
gr[1] = "A";
cr[1] = 4;
gr[2] = "A-";
cr[2] = 3.66;
gr[3] = "B+";
cr[3] = 3.33;
gr[4] = "B";
cr[4] = 3;
gr[5] = "B-";
cr[5] = 2.66;
gr[6] = "C+";
cr[6] = 2.33;
gr[7] = "C";
cr[7] = 2;
gr[8] = "C-";
cr[8] = 1.66;
gr[9] = "D";
cr[9] = 1;
gr[10] = "F";
cr[10] = 0;
// retrieve user input
ingr[0] = document.GPACalcForm.GR1.value;
ingr[1] = document.GPACalcForm.GR2.value;
```

```
ingr[2] = document.GPACalcForm.GR3.value;
ingr[3] = document.GPACalcForm.GR4.value;
ingr[4] = document.GPACalcForm.GR5.value;
ingr[5] = document.GPACalcForm.GR6.value;
ingr[6] = document.GPACalcForm.GR7.value;
ingr[7] = document.GPACalcForm.GR8.value;
incr[0] = document.GPACalcForm.CR1.value;
incr[1] = document.GPACalcForm.CR2.value;
incr[2] = document.GPACalcForm.CR3.value;
incr[3] = document.GPACalcForm.CR4.value;
incr[4] = document.GPACalcForm.CR5.value;
incr[5] = document.GPACalcForm.CR6.value;
ingr[6] = document.GPACalcForm.GR7.value;
ingr[7] = document.GPACalcForm.GR8.value;
// Calculate GPA
var allgr =0;
var allcr = 0;
var gpa = 0;
for (var x = 0; x < 5 + 3; x++)
{
if (ingr[x] == "") break;
// if (isNaN(parseInt(incr[x]))) alert("Error- You did not enter a numeric credits value
for Class If the class is worth 0 credits then enter the number 0 in the field.");
var validgrcheck = 0;
for (var xx = 0; xx < grcount; xx++)
{
if (ingr[x] == gr[xx])
{
allgr = allgr + (parseInt(incr[x],10) * cr[xx]);
allcr = allcr + parseInt(incr[x],10);
```

```
    validgrcheck = 1;
    break;
    }
  }
  if (validgrcheck == 0)
  {
    alert("Error- Could not recognize the grade entered for Class " + eval(x + 1) + ".
Please use standard college grades in the form of A A- B+ ...F.");
    return 0;
  }
}

// this if-check prevents a divide by zero error
if (allcr == 0)
{
  alert("Error- You did not enter any credit values! GPA = N/A");
  return 0;
}

gpa = allgr / allcr;

alert("GPA = " + eval(gpa));

return 0;
}

//-->

</SCRIPT>
```

**Output:** Simple standard calculator

```
<FORM NAME="Calc">
<TABLE BORDER=4>
<TR>
<TD>
<INPUT TYPE="text" NAME="Input" Size="16">
<br>
</TD>
</TR>
<TR>
<TD>
<INPUT TYPE="button" NAME="one" VALUE=" 1 " OnClick="Calc.Input.value
+= '1'">
<INPUT TYPE="button" NAME="two" VALUE=" 2 " OnCLick="Calc.Input.value
+= '2'">
<INPUT TYPE="button" NAME="three" VALUE=" 3 " OnClick="Calc.Input.
value += '3'">
<INPUT TYPE="button" NAME="plus" VALUE=" + " OnClick="Calc.Input.value
+= ' + '">
<br>
<INPUT TYPE="button" NAME="four" VALUE=" 4 " OnClick="Calc.Input.value
+= '4'">
<INPUT TYPE="button" NAME="five" VALUE=" 5 " OnCLick="Calc.Input.value
+= '5'">
<INPUT TYPE="button" NAME="six" VALUE=" 6 " OnClick="Calc.Input.value
+= '6'">
<INPUT TYPE="button" NAME="minus" VALUE=" - " OnClick="Calc.Input.
value += ' - '">
<br>
```

```
<INPUT TYPE="button" NAME="seven" VALUE=" 7 " OnClick="Calc.Input.
value += '7'">\
<INPUT TYPE="button" NAME="eight" VALUE=" 8 " OnCLick="Calc.Input.
value += '8'">
<INPUT TYPE="button" NAME="nine" VALUE=" 9 " OnClick="Calc.Input.value
+= '9'">
<INPUT TYPE="button" NAME="times" VALUE=" x " OnClick="Calc.Input.
value += ' * '">
<br>
<INPUT TYPE="button" NAME="clear" VALUE=" c " OnClick="Calc.Input.value
= '">
<INPUT TYPE="button" NAME="zero" VALUE=" 0 " OnClick="Calc.Input.value
+= '0'">
<INPUT TYPE="button" NAME="DoIt" VALUE=" = " OnClick="Calc.Input.
value = eval(Calc.Input.value)">
<INPUT TYPE="button" NAME="div" VALUE=" / " OnClick="Calc.Input.value
+= ' / '">
<br>
</TD>
</TR>
</TABLE>
</FORM>
```

**Output:** Text box that allows user to paste text in, and it will calculate how many
words are in it

```
<form method="POST" name="wordcount">
<script language="JavaScript">
```

```
function countit(){


var formcontent=document.wordcount.wordcount2.value
formcontent=formcontent.split(" ")
document.wordcount.wordcount3.value=formcontent.length
}
</script>
<table border="0" cellspacing="0" cellpadding="0">
<tr>
<td width="100%"><textarea rows="12" name="wordcount2" cols="60" wrap="virtual"></textarea></td>
</tr>
<tr>
<td width="100%"><div align="right"><p><input type="button" value="Calculate Words"
onClick="countit()"> <input type="text" name="wordcount3" size="20"></p>
</tr>
</table>
</form>
```

## Javacripts
### *Text Effects*
**Output:** Makes your text look like a rollercoaster

```
<script>

var fs=1
var direction="right"
```

```
function rollertext(whichone){
var thetext=whichone
for (i=0;i<thetext.length;i++){
document.write(thetext.charAt(i).fontsize(fs))

if (fs<7&&direction=="right")
fs++
else if (fs==7){
direction="left"
fs—
}
else if (fs==1){
direction="right"
fs++
}
else if (fs>1&&direction=="left")
fs—

}
}
//Change below text to your own
rollertext("Cybronics!")
</script>
```

## Output: makes your output look like neon lights

```
<h2>

<script language="JavaScript1.2">
```

```
var message="Welcome to Cybronics!"
var neonbasecolor="gray"
var neontextcolor="yellow"
var flashspeed=100 //in milliseconds


///No need to edit below this line/////

var n=0
if (document.all){
document.write('<font color="'+neonbasecolor+'">')
for (m=0;m<message.length;m++)
document.write('<span id="neonlight">'+message.charAt(m)+'</span>')
document.write('</font>')

//cache reference to neonlight array
var tempref=document.all.neonlight
}
else
document.write(message)

function neon(){


//Change all letters to base color
if (n==0){
for (m=0;m<message.length;m++)
tempref[m].style.color=neonbasecolor
}
```

```
//cycle through and change individual letters to neon color
tempref[n].style.color=neontextcolor

if (n<tempref.length-1)
n++
else{
n=0
clearInterval(flashing)
setTimeout("beginneon()",1500)
return
}
}

function beginneon(){
if (document.all)
flashing=setInterval("neon()",flashspeed)
}
beginneon()


</script>
</h2>
```

# GLOSSARY

## WORDS WERTH KNOWIN

The following are a few typical, but important words to know on and about the Internet. Readers, who would like to know even more words, might want to buy an online dictionary. To know what the heck they are talking about online, this list will be a good starting point. The author created these definitions.

- *AFK*—Away from keyboard. A user is not currently at ones computers to respond.
- *AKA*—Also known as
- *Alias*—a nickname that refers to a person or group
- *Anchor*—marks the start and end of hypertext links
- *Applet*—a small java program that is embedded in a webpage.
- *Archie*—A program used to find files on the Internet, which can later be downloaded.
- *Archive*—a collection of files stored on a computer network
- *Article*—A name applied to a message posted on a newsgroup.
- *Authentication*—a security measure to check a user's identity
- *Bandwidth*—The amount of data that can be sent through a network connection
- *Baud*—how many bits sent or received per second

- *BBL*—Be back later
- *BBS*—a dial up meeting system
- *Bit*—the smallest unit of computerized data.
- *Blatherer*—Someone that talks and talks; uses many words.
- *Bookmark*—An online "page marker"; this allows you to come back to an online site conveniently.
- *Booted*—Being kicked offline, normally due to a violation or reported violation.
- *Bot*—NOT A PROGRAM; This is a simple device that is taught to look for something, or to follow a specific instruction.
- *Bps*—bits per second: measurement of how fast data is moved from one place to another.
- *BRB*—Be right back.
- *Browser*—A utility that allows you to " browse" and "surf" the Internet.
- *BTW*—By the way
- *Byte*—a set of bits
- *Clickable image map*—a graphic that has assorted hyperlinks on various portions of the image.
- *Client*—a remote computer connected to a server
- *Cookie*—a piece of information sent from the browser back to the server
- *Cyberspace*—term applied to refer to the digital world
- *Dedicated line*—a communications line that has a permanent connection to the Internet
- *Domain name*—The identifier to an Internet site

- *Dood*—The online equivalent to a <<California dude.>>
- *Download*—a data transfer from one computer to another
- *DSL*—digital subscriber line
- *Email*—Electronic mail; Sending electronic messages across the Internet.
- *Encryption*—A method of making data unreadable by everyone but the receiver
- *Ethernet*—a method of connecting computers on a local area network (LAN)
- *FAQ*—Stands for: Frequently Asked Questions; normally contains responses to questions made by users.
- *Finder*—A utility that is used to "find" information on the Internet.
- *Finger*—A utility that is used to find information on the Internet.
- *Fire wall*—File system protected against unauthorized users
- *Flame*—Insults and abuses towards another online user.
- *Freeware*—free software
- *FTP*—File Transfer Protocol; Used for transmitting files across the Internet.
- *G2g*—Got to Go
- *Gateway*—A computer that is used to connect large groups of computers to the Internet, " Gateway to the Internet."
- *Gigabyte*—1000 megabytes
- *GMTA*—Great minds think alike.
- *Gopher*—A program that is used to "tunnel" between different networks in search of information.

- *Hit*—Referring to the act of accessing an html page
- *Home page*—the first page on a website
- *Host*—a computer that acts as a server
- *HTML*—HyperText Markup Language; The language used to create World Wide Web documents. (The language that is being taken over by Java; See JAVA.)
- *HTTP*—the most important protocol on the WWW
- *Hyperlink*—links to html documents that are usually clickable
- *Hypermedia*—the multimedia files available on the internet
- *IMHO*—in my humble opinion
- *Internet*—The online network of mass information and pages, available to users by online services.
- *Intranet*—a private network inside an organization
- *IP*—Information Provider/ Internet Protocol, Rules that computers have to obey to communicate on the Internet.
- *IRC*—Internet Relay Chat; Something that is becoming obsolete, but allows real time conversation with other online users.
- *ISDN*—Integrated Services Digital Network: lines with 2 channels that can carry information at 128kps.
- *Internet service provider*—a company that provides a variety of accounts to access the Internet
- *JAVA*—A new electronic language created by Sun Microsystems; Allows even more extensive multimedia options.
- *Jughead*—Program used for searching on the gopher servers.
- *K*—Ok or Okay.

- *Keyword*—Typically found on a well-known Internet provider; Shortcuts that are used by typing in a known name to bring up a specific online area.
- *KW*—(see Keyword.)
- *LAN*—Local Area Network; A connection of computer via cables to transfer data.
- *Login/Log On*—To sign online, normally by typing in ones screen name (or username) and password.
- *Logoff/logout*—to sign offline
- *LoL*—Laugh out loud or laughing out loud.
- *Lurker*—Someone that reads without posting information; an online information abuser.
- *Mail bomb*—flooding a person's email account with junk messages
- *Mail bot*—an email server that automatically responds to information
- *Mailing-list*—A subscribed list to receive emails from a particular user or organization.
- *Modem*—a device for translating digital data of computers into analog signals over phone lines.
- *Navigate*—Move around or negotiate the WWW
- *NET*—A shorthand notations for the Internet.
- *Net God*—Longtime, omniscient, online users. (What Doogie and Metafire are)
- *Netiquette*—rules that guide the online world
- *Netizen*—a citizen of the online world or Internet

- *Network*—A connection of computers, by some means, allowing transmission of data.
- *Newbie*—Someone new to the online world who often recieves abuse from Net Gods
- *Newsgroup*—Discussion group online.
- *Node*—any single computer connected to a network
- *Online*—when a user is connected to the network or internet
- *Password*—a combination used to login to information.
- *Ping*—A diagnostic program used to see if another computer is present.
- *Plug-in*—a small piece of software that adds features to a larger piece of software
- *POP*—Point of Presence; Local phone numbers maintained by Internet providers.
- *Posting*—a single message entered into a network communications system
- *PPP*—Point-to-Point Protocol; a type of online access; a direct access to the NET.
- *Protocol*—a specification that describes how computers talk to each other
- *ROFL*—Rolling on the floor laughing.
- *Router*—A piece of hardware or software that connects a local network to the Internet.
- *Screen Name*—(SN) Online name used to login and use the Internet via an Internet Provider.

- *Script*—program that runs on a webserver and requests input from the user.
- *Scrolling*—Typing the same thing over and over again in chat. Normally results in being booted offline.
- *Search Engine*—A utility on the Internet that allows one to find information by typing in keywords.
- *Server*—a host computer that answers requests from other computers.
- *Shareware*—a software trial available for download on the Internet
- *Slip*—Serial Line Internet Protocol; a direct type of online access, requiring TCP/IP software.
- *SN*—(see screen name.)
- *Spamming*—to post an excess of irrelevant matter.
- *Surfer*—An online dood.
- *System Response*—the time in which it takes for the service provider respond to a users requests.
- *SR*—(see system Response.)
- *T1, T3 Lines*—Leased telephone lines that connect large LANs to Internet at high speeds.
- *TCP*—Transmission Control Protocol; (See IP)
- *Telnet*—A communications protocol that allows a user to log onto another distant computer.
- *Terminal* –a device that allows commands to be sent to a computer located elsewhere

- *TOS*—Terms of Service; the online "code" which is not to be broken; If broken might result in being "booted" or losing ones account.

- *Under construction*—a term used to describe that a site is still being developed

- *Unix*—A complex and powerful (often confusing and scary) operating system. This is often used on large network machines used by engineers.

- *URL*—Uniform Resource Locator. The "address" of a WWW page.

- *Username*—a name assigned to users on a computer network

- *Usenet*—A network featuring many discussion groups.

- *UserName*—another term applied to Screen Name. (See Screen Name.)

- *Viewer*—a browser

- *Violation*—An action, which violated the TOS; normally results in being booted. (see Booted.)

- *Virtual*—lifelike material in cyberspace

- *WAIS*—Wide Area Information Server; an electronic "librarian."

- *WB*—Welcome back.

- *Webmaster*—the person responsible for maintaining a website

- *WWW*—The World Wide Web, a network of online pages containing many multimedia features. These pages are linked together, resulting in a mass network enabling users to search and access data around the world

- *Zip/Unzip*—compressing/decompressing files using software

# APPENDICES

## Appendix I
*History of the Internet*

| | |
|---|---|
| 1958 | President Eisenhower requests funds to create ARPA (Advance Research Projects Agency. |
| Oct. 1965 | First Network Experiment: Directed by Larry Roberts at MIT Lincoln Lab, two computers talked to each other using packet-switching technology. |
| Dec. 1966 | ARPA project begins |
| Sept. 1, 1969 | First ARPANet component is installed at UCLA |
| Oct. 1, 1969 | Second component is installed at Stanford |
| Nov. 1, 1969 | Third node installed at University of California, Santa Barbara. |
| Dec. 1, 1969 | Fourth node installed at University of Utah. |
| March 1970 | Fifth node installed at BBN, across the country in Cambridge, Mass. March 1972 First basic email programs arise and use of the "@" symbol |

| | |
|---|---|
| March 1973 | First ARPANET international connections to University College of London (England) and NORSAR (Norway). |
| 1976 | -Apple Computer is founded by Steve Jobs and Steve Wozniak.<br>-Queen Elizabeth II sends out an e-mail. 1981 IBM announces its first Personal Computer. Microsoft creates DOS |
| 1983 | Cisco Systems founded. |
| Nov. 1983 | Domain Names are designed. Examples: .edu, .gov, .com, .mil, .org, .net, and .int are created. |
| 1984 | William Gibson writes "Neuromancer." Coins the term "cyberspace" |
| March 15, 1985 | Symbolic.com becomes the first registered domain. |
| 1986 | 5000 hosts on ARPAnet/Internet |
| 1987 | -10,000 hosts on the Internet.<br>-2.5 Million PCs made |
| 1989 | -100,000 hosts on Internet.<br>-McAfee Associates founded; anti-virus software available for free. |
| 1990 | ARPAnet ends. Tim Berners-Lee creates the World Wide Web. |
| 1992 | "Surfing the Internet" is coined by Jean Armour Polly. |
| April 1994 | -Netscape is founded. |

|  | -Jeff Bezos writes the business plan for Amazon.com.<br>-Java's first public demonstration. |
| Dec. 1994 | Microsoft licenses technology from Spyglass to create Web browser for Windows 95 |
| May 23, 1995 | Sun Microsystems releases Java. |
| August 24, 1995 | Windows 95 released. |
| 1996 | Domain name tv.com sold to CNET for $15,000. Browser wars begin. Netscape and Microsoft two biggest players. |
| 1997 | business.com sold for $150,000. |
| 1999 | -AOL buys Netscape<br>-Browsers wars declared over; Netscape and Microsoft share almost 100% of browser market.<br>-Microsoft declared a monopoly by US District Court |
| Jan. 10, 2000 | AOL Merges with Time-Warner. |

## Appendix II
*Error Messages*

| 400 Bad File Request | Usually means the syntax used in the url is incorrect specifically lower/uppercase letters and punctuation. |

**401 Unauthorized**

Wrong password, or the server is looking for an encryption key that it is not receiving.

**403 Forbidden/Access Denied**

Similar to 401, This means there is special permission needed to access the site: a password and/or username.

**404 File Not Found**

Server cannot find the file you requested. File has either been moved or deleted, or you entered the wrong url or document name. Look at the url. If a word looks misspelled, try correcting it. If that doesn't work backtrack by deleting information between each backslash, until you come to a page on that site that isn't a 404 error.

**408 Request Timeout**

The client stopped the request before the server finished retrieving it. Most likely it was taking too long to receive the information

**500 Internal Error**

Couldn't find a document because of server configuration. System administrator should be contacted.

**501 Not Implemented**

Web server doesn't support a requested feature

**502 Service Temporarily** — **Overloaded** Congestion; too many connections; high traffic. Keep trying until the page loads.

**503 Service Unavailable** — This means the server is busy, the site may have moved, or you lost your dial-up Internet connection.

**File Contains No Data** — Page is there but is not showing anything.

**Bad File Request** — Your browser does not accept the form that it is receiving.

**Failed DNS Lookup** — The Domain Name Server can't translate your domain request into a valid Internet address. Server may be busy or down, or an incorrect url was entered.

**Host Unavailable** — The host server is down. Hit reload or go to the site at a later time.

**Unable to Locate Host** — Host server is down, Internet connection is lost, or url is incorrect.

## Appednix III
*Search Engines*

- **Alta Vista**        www.altavist.com
- **Ask Jeeves**        www.askjeeves.com
- **Excite**        www.excite.com
- **Go**        www.go.com
- **Google**        www.google.com
- **GoTo**        www.goto.com
- **HotBot**        www.hotbot.com
- **LookSmart**        www.looksmart.com
- **Lycos**        www.lycos.com
- **NorthernLight**        www.northernlight.com

## Appendix IV
*Anti-Virus Tips*

1. **Do not open** any files attached to an email from any unknown or suspicious source

2. **Do not open** any files attached to an email unless you know what the files are, even if it appears to come from a friend. Some viruses replicate themselves and spread throughout email or buddylists. Better safe than sorry and confirm what the files are before opening them.

3. **Do not open** any files attached to an email if the subject line is questionable or unexpected. If you need to, save the file to a remote drive.

4. **Delete chain emails and junk email.** Do not forward or reply to any chain mail. These types of email are considered spam, and sometimes contain viruses and clog network traffic

5. **Do not download** any files from strangers.

6. **Exercise caution** when downloading files from the Internet. Make sure that the source is a legitimate and reputable one. Use an anti-virus program to check the files on the download site. If uncertain, don't download the file.

7. **Update your anti-virus software regularly.** Over 500 viruses are discovered each month.

8. **Back up your files on a regular basis.** If a virus destroys your files, at least you can replace them with your back-up copy. You should store copies of your files on remote or removable media or drives.

9. When in doubt, **always err on the side of caution** and do not open, download, or execute any files or email attachments.

10. **Always** report viruses to your Internet or email provider.

## Appendix V
*Virus Terms*

*Anti-antivirus Virus*—Virus that attacks or disables anti-virus software

*Anti-virus Software*—software that scans a computer's memory and drives for viruses.

*Armored Virus*—A virus that tries to prevent analysts from examining its code

*Back Door*—A feature built into a program that allows special privileges usually denied to user in a program.

*Backup*—a duplicate copy of data made for archiving to prevent loss or damage of information

*Bimodal virus*—A virus that infects both boot records and files

*Brute Force Attack*—An attack made by trial and error to achieve a password

*Bug*—Unintentional fault in a program

*Cavity Virus*—A virus that overwrites a part of its host file without increasing the length of the file

*Clean*—The act of removing viruses

*Cluster virus*—A virus that modifies the directy table entries so the virus starts before any other program

*Companion Virus*—Viruses that create a COM file which has a higher priority that an EXE file with the same name.

*Compromise*—Accessing information without authorization

*Direct Action Virus*—A virus that works immediately to load itself into memory, and the unload itself.

*Dropper*—A carrier file that installs a virus onto a system

*Encrypted Virus*—A virus with a code that begins with a decryption algorithm and continues with encrypted code for the remainder of the virus.

*Encryption*—Scrambling of data so it is difficult to interpret or unscramble

*Fast Infector*—Infect not only executed programs but also any programs that are open at the time

*File Viruses*—Usuall replace or attach themselves to Com and EXE files.

*Hole*—vulnerability in the design of a computer program

*Logic Bomb*—Type of Trojan horse that executes when specific conditions are present

*Macro Virus*—is a malicious macro (miniprogram)

*Mailbomb*—Excessive amounts of junk email received to a person's account via a program

*Malware*—A generic term used to describe malicious software

*Memory-Resident Virus*—A virus that stays in the memory after it is execute and infects other programs when conditions are met

*Mutating Virus*—A virus that changes or mutates as it progresses through the host's files.

*Overwriting virus*—A virus that copies its code over its host's file data, destroying programs

*Password attacks*—is an attempt to obtain or hack a user's password.

*Password Sniffing*—A program that captures and logs passwords as they are used over networks

*Payload*—The effects produced by a virus attack

*Piggy back*—Gaining unauthorized access to a system via an authorized user's connection

*Polymorphic virus*—Creates varied copies of itself as a way to avoid detection from anti-virus software

*Program infector*—a virus that infects other program files once an infected application is executed

*Replication*—Process of a virus making copies of itself in order to carry out more infections

*Resident Virus*—Loads itself into memory and remains inactive into an event triggers its attack

*Rogue Program*—a term used to describe a program that was written with the intent to damage other programs or data

*Scanner*—A virus detection program that searches for viruses on a user's computer

*Self garbling viruses*—A virus that attempts to hide from anti-virus software by garbling its own code

*Slow infect*—A virus that are in active memory and only infect new files or files that are modified thereafter

*Sniffer*—a program that monitors network traffic

*Sparse Virus*—A virus that uses conditions before infecting files

*Stealth Virus*—A virus that attempts to conceal its presence from anti-virus software.

*Time bomb*—An action triggered at a specific date or time

*Triggered Event*—an action that sets off a virus on a specific condition or event

*Trojan horse program*—is a malicious program that pretends to be a regular application. Trojans usually gain passwords and other information from a users computer form within

*Tunneling*—A technique designed to prevent anti-virus programs from working correctly

*Vaccination*—a technique used by anti-virus program to store information about files in order to notify the user when changes occur

*Variant*—a modified version of a virus

*Virus*—a computer program that is capable of attaching itself to disks or files and replicating itself throughout a system.

*Worm*—Parasitic computer program that replicate. They don't damage files, however replicate them and send them to another user

*Zoo*—a collection of viruses used for testing by researchers

*Zoo virus*—a virus that exists in the collection of researchers and has never infected a real world computer system

www.ingramcontent.com/pod-product-compliance
Lightning Source LLC
Chambersburg PA
CBHW051255050326
40689CB00007B/1208